THE **YELLOW** AND
HIGHLY
DANGEROUS
JOKEBOOK

What is yellow, then green,
then yellow, then green?
*A banana that works
part-time as a cuc...*

What's left after a lawn-mower
runs over a canary?
Shredded Tweet.

What's yellow and highly dangerous?
Chop sueycide.

Other Jokebooks from Mammoth

The Green and Hairy Joke Book
by Gus Berry
The Creepy Crawly Joke Book
by Katie Wales
Love & Kisses
A light-hearted book for your Valentine
by Paul Hooper
The Holiday Joke Book
by Katie Wales

THE **YELLOW** AND

HIGHLY

DANGEROUS

JOKEBOOK

GUS BERRY
with cartoons by Tony Blundell

MAMMOTH

First published 1989 by Magnet
Reissued 1989 by Mammoth
an imprint of Mandarin Paperbacks
Michelin House, 81 Fulham Road, London SW3 6RB
Text copyright © 1989 Martyn Forrester
Illustrations copyright © 1989 Tony Blundell

ISBN 0 7497 0221 4

Printed and bound in Great Britain by
Cox & Wyman Ltd, Reading

What's yellow and highly dangerous?

A bunch of angry bananas.

How do you stop a herd of bananas from charging?
Take away their credit cards.

What is yellow, has one bionic eye, and fights crime?
The Six Million Dollar Banana.

What is yellow, then green, then yellow, then green?
A banana that works part-time as a cucumber.

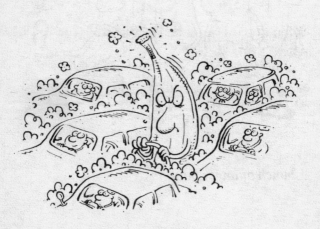

What's yellow and goes 'Beep! Beep!'?
A banana in a traffic jam.

What is made from two banana skins?
A pair of slippers.

What do you get if you cross two bananas
with a tomato?
A pair of red slippers.

What is the best thing to put into banana pie?
Your teeth!

How can you tell a banana from an aspirin?
Bananas come in bunches.

Why don't bananas have dandruff?
Did you ever see a banana with hair?

What's yellow, washable, dries quickly
and needs no ironing?
A drip-dry banana.

What's yellow and goes at 60mph?
A banana on a motorbike.

What's yellow and comes out of the
trees at 200mph?
A jet-propelled banana.

What's yellow and grows in an apple tree?
A stupid banana.

What's yellow and has twenty-two legs?
Banana United!

Why don't they grow bananas any
longer?
Because they're long enough already.

What's yellow and hums?
An electric banana.

Knock, knock.
– *Who's there?*

Banana.
– *Banana who?*

Knock, knock.
– *Who's there?*

Banana.
– *Banana who?*

Knock, knock.
– *Who's there?*

Orange.
– *Orange who?*

Orange you glad I didn't say banana?

What's yellow and goes round and round and round?
A banana in a washing machine.

If a crocodile makes shoes, what does a banana make?
Slippers.

Why didn't the banana snore?
Because it was afraid of waking up the rest of the bunch.

Why did the strawberry jelly wobble?
Because it saw the banana milk-shake.

Why did the banana go to the doctor?
Because it wasn't peeling very well.

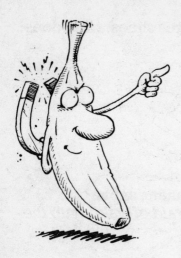

What's yellow
and points
north?
*A magnetic
banana.*

What's yellow
and points
south?
*A stupid
magnetic
banana.*

What's yellow and goes click- click?
A ball- point banana

**What do you get if you cross a yellow
fruit with a bell?**
A banana that can peel itself.

**How do you stop a banana from
ripening on Sunday?**
Pick it on Saturday.

**What's yellow and goes
slam- slam- slam- slam?**
A four- door banana.

What is a banana skin most used for?
To keep the banana together.

**Why did the banana
go out with
the prune?**
*Because he couldn't
find a date.*

What's yellow and goes up and down?
A banana in a lift.

What's yellow
and goes
thump-squish,
thump-squish?
A banana with one wet plimsoll.

What's enormous and yellow and says
'Fe-fi-fo-fum'?
A giant banana.

What's yellow, wears a cape, and fights
crime?
Superbanana.

What's yellow
and square?
*A banana in
disguise.*

What's yellow and 440 metres high?
The Empire State Banana.

What's yellow
and wears
a mask?
The Lone Banana.

What do you get if you cross a banana with
a skunk?
A skunk with a yellow streak down its back.

What did the banana do when the
chimpanzee chased it?
The banana split.

What do you get if you cross a banana with
a comedian?
Peels of laughter.

What's the best time to pick bananas?
When the farmer is in bed.

Why are apples red?
If they were yellow they'd be lemons.

What do you get if you cross an apple with a Christmas tree?
A pineapple.

What's an apple that is small and yellow at picking time?
A failure.

What's red and miserable and covered in custard?
Apple grumble.

What is yellow and highly dangerous?
A herd of stampeding bananas.

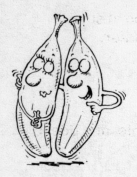

What did the
handsome boy
banana say
to the pretty
girl banana?
'You appeal to me.'

What's big and yellow and lives in
Scotland?
The Loch Ness Banana.

What's yellow and good at sums?
A banana with a calculator.

What's yellow, washable, and doesn't need ironing?
A drip-dry banana.

Why is a banana skin like a pullover?
Because it's easy to slip on.

Where was the first banana found?
In a tree.

What is worse than a redskin on the warpath?
A banana skin on the footpath.

What do you get if you cross a yellow
fruit with a Greek singer?
Banana Mouskouri.

What is the
hardest thing
to eat?
*A banana
sideways.*

What's yellow has four wheels and is
eaten by monkeys?
Bananas – I lied about the wheels.

Why can't a banana be
twelve inches long?
*Because then it
would be a foot.*

What would you do if you found a blue
banana?
Try to cheer it up.

What do you get hanging from banana
trees?
Aching arms.

What's yellow and jumps up and down?
A banana at a disco.

What's long and yellow and shaped like a banana?
A banana.

What's long and yellow and says 'Pardon'?
A polite banana with hiccups.

'What's the difference between a £5 pound note and a banana?'
'I don't know.'
'You couldn't lend me a banana, could you?'

What do you
get if you
cross a rug
with a banana?
A carpet slipper.

What's the difference between stork and butter?
Butter can't stand on one leg.

What's the best butter in the world?
A goat.

What's yellow and highly dangerous?
A canary with a machine- gun.

What's left after a lawn- mower runs over a canary?
Shredded Tweet.

What do you get if you cross a cat with a canary?
A satisfied cat and a dead canary.

What do you get if you cross an elephant with a canary?
A very messy cage.

Man: This canary you sold me has a broken leg.
Pet shop owner: *You only asked for a good singer – I didn't know you wanted him to dance as well.*

Man: Can I have a canary for my wife please?
Pet shop owner: I'm sorry sir, we don't do swaps.

What succeeds like nothing else?
A toothless canary.

What bird cannot fly as high as you can jump?
A canary in a cage.

What do you do with sick canaries?
Give them tweetment.

What's yellow and has a wingspan of fifteen metres?
A two and a half ton canary.

What's yellow, has twenty-four legs, and sings?
Twelve canaries.

DEBBIE: I have a canary that can do something I can't.
EMMA: What's that?
DEBBIE: Take a bath in a teacup.

What's yellow and highly dangerous?
Chop sueycide

What's yellow and fills fields with music?
Popcorn.

What's small and furry and cuts corn?
A combine hamster.

What did the little corn say to momma corn?
'Where's popcorn?'

Why shouldn't you tell secrets in a vegetable garden?
Because corn has ears.

Why was the farmer hopping mad?
Because somebody stepped on his corn.

Where did the baby ear of corn come from?
The stalk brought him.

Why was the corn stalk angry with the farmer?
The farmer kept pulling its ears.

Why did the idiot put corn in his shoes?
Because of his pigeon toes.

Two ears of corn were running up a hill.
What were they when they got to the top?
Puffed wheat.

Lemon

*What's yellow
and goes round
and round and
round?
A long-playing
lemon.*

*What's yellow, full of seeds, and looks
like half a lemon?
The other half of the lemon.*

What's yellow, sour, and goes 'Splutter,
splutter, splutter'?
A lemon running out of juice.

What's cowardly, thin, and full of
noodles?
Chicken soup.

What do you get if you cross a cowardly
cow with a pullover?
A yellow jersey.

What is yellow and highly dangerous?
Kamikaze custard.

What's yellow and prickly?
A cowardy custard hedgehog.

What's the better fighter, a banana or a chicken?
A banana - it's no chicken.

What happened to the criminal banana?
It was taken into custardy.

What's yellow and stupid?
Thick custard.

Why do elephants paint their toe-nails yellow?
So they can hide upside down in custard.

How can you tell when there's an elephant in your custard?
When it's especially lumpy.

If you have a referee in boxing, a referee in football, and a referee in rugby, what do you have in bowls?
Custard.

Lady to a tramp who's asked for a meal: *Do you like cold custard?*
Tramp: *I love it, lady.*
Lady: *Well call back later, it's very hot right now.*

What's yellow and wobbly and wears dark glasses?
A bowl of custard in disguise.

What happened to the man who couldn't tell putty from custard?
His windows fell out.

What's red outside, yellow inside, and very crowded?
A bus of custard.

Why did the man
have to go to
hospital after
the custard fell
on his head?
It was in a tin.

A man saw a gardener pushing a wheel-
barrow full of manure. 'Where are you going
with that?' he asked. *'Going to put it on my
goosberries,'* said the gardener. 'Suit yourself,'
said the man, 'I usually put custard on
mine.'

What's yellow and wobbly
and comes at you
from all sides?
Stereophonic custard.

What's yellow and wobbly and goes round
and round?
A bowl of long-playing custard.

What's yellow and wobbly and moves along
the bottom of the sea?
A bowl of custard in a submarine.

Canteen lady: Do you want more of this
custard?
Boy: *No thanks, I'm too young to die.*

Boy: Have you got any custard left?
Canteen lady: *Yes.*
Boy: Well you shouldn't have made so much
then.

Boy: Can I have some custard please?
Canteen lady: *One lump or two?*

1st girl: Here, try some of this banana custard I've just made.
2nd girl: *Ugh! It's horrible!*
1st girl: You've no taste – it definitely says in my cookery book that this recipe is delicious.

What's yellow and wobbly and wears sunglasses?
A bowl of custard on holiday.

What's yellow and wobbly and has four wheels?
A bowl of custard on a skateboard.

What's yellow and wobbly and has eight wheels?
A bowl of custard on roller skates.

What's yellow and wobbly and goes
bang?
A bowl of custard in a minefield.

What's yellow and wobbly inside and
white outside?
A custard sandwich.

What's yellow and wobbly and croaks?
A bowl of custard with a cold.

What do you get if you cross a sheep, a
dog and a bowl of custard?
Collie-wobbles.

What's 300 metres tall, weighs 7,620
tons, and is made of custard?
The Trifle Tower.

What's yellow and highly dangerous?
An Eggs-ocet missile.

What is yellow and flat and goes around
at 33 1/3 revolutions per minute?
A long-playing omelette.

What's yellow and white and travels at
100mph?
A train-driver's egg sandwich.

What do you get if you cross a hen with
a poodle?
Pooched eggs.

What do you get if you cross a hen with
an electric organ?
Hammond eggs.

Have you heard the one about the three
boiled eggs?
Two bad!

Why did the egg go into the jungle?
Because it was an egg-splorer.

If an egg came floating down the River Thames, where would it have come from?
A chicken.

What's the best way to make an egg roll?
Push it down a hill.

What do you get if you cross a chicken with a kangaroo?
Pouched eggs.

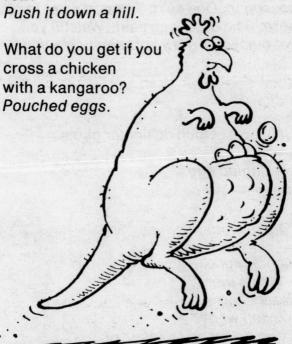

Knock, knock.
– *Who's there?*
Egbert.
– *Egbert who?*
Egbert no bacon.

There were two eggs boiling in a saucepan. One said, 'Phew, it's hot in here.' The other egg said, *'Wait till you get out, you'll get your head bashed in.'*

What sort of food do fighter pilots prefer?
Scrambled eggs.

Knock, knock.
– *Who's there?*
Exam.
– *Exam who?*
Eggs, ham and cheese.

Who conquered half the world, laying
eggs along the way?
Attila the Hen.

Doctor: I'm
afraid you only
have three
more minutes
to live.
Patient: Is there nothing you can do for
me?
Doctor: I could boil you an egg.

'Waiter, these eggs are bad.'
'Don't blame me, I only laid the table.'

What's a mischievous egg called?
A practical yolker.

What's the best way to make an egg roll?
Push it downhill.

How do Daleks deal with eggs?
They eggs- terminate them.

What do you get if you give chickens whisky?
Scotch eggs.

What's yellow and highly dangerous?

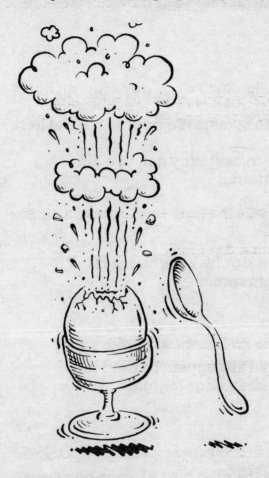

A big eggs–plosion.

Who wrote Great Eggspectations?
Charles Chickens.

Customer: Two soggy eggs on burnt toast, please.
Café owner: We can't serve that here, sir.
Customer: Why not, you did yesterday.

How do chickens start a race?
From scratch.

What are eggshells used for?
To keep eggs together.

Where's the best place to buy eggs?
Henley.

What tells jokes and lays eggs?
A comedi-hen.

What do you get if you cross a piece of toast
with an egg and an eiderdown?
Breakfast in bed.

What do you get
if you cross a hen
with a banjo?
*A chicken that
plucks itself.*

What do you get if you cross a hen with
some gunpowder?
An eggs-plosion.

Why did the chicken run onto the football
pitch?
Because the referee blew for a foul.

How does a wally make scrambled eggs?
*He holds the pan and gets two friends to shake
him violently.*

'Doctor, doctor, my tongue is as yellow as custard and my legs are as wobbly as jelly.'
'Don't worry – you're just a trifle ill.'

'Doctor, doctor, this banana diet isn't working on me.'
'Stop scratching and come down from the curtains.'

'Doctor, doctor, I've got bananas growing out of my ears.'
'Good gracious, how did that happen?'
'I don't know, I planted apples.'

What's yellow and sneaks around the kitchen?
Custard spies.

What's yellow and round and 5 miles in circumference?
The Great Ball of China.

What's yellow,
comes from Peru,
and is totally unknown?
Euston Bear.

What's yellow and never talks to anyone?
A lemon sole.

What's yellow and stays hot in the fridge?
Mustard.

What's yellow, full of holes, and holds water?
A wet sponge.

What's yellow, weighs 4 tons, and has a blocked trunk?
An elephant drowning in a bowl of custard.

'Doctor, doctor, I feel like a yellow snooker ball.'
'Well get to the back of the queue (cue).'

'Doctor, doctor, for the last ten years my brother has believed he is a hen.'
'Goodness gracious, why didn't you come to me sooner?'
'We needed the eggs.'

What do you get if you cross a daffodil with a calculator?
A flower with square roots.

'Doctor, doctor, my mother thinks I'm crazy because I prefer yellow socks to grey ones.'
'What's crazy about that? So do I.'
'Really? How do you like them – fried or boiled?'

'Doctor, doctor, I feel like a banana.'
'So do I – get me one too.'

'Doctor, doctor, I feel like custard'
'Sit down, man, and don't be so thick.'

Why don't grapefruit tie their own shoelaces?
If you had a shape like a grapefruit, you couldn't see your feet either.

How can you tell that strawberries are lazy?
They spend their entire lives in bed.

What is an overweight pumpkin called?

A plumpkin.

Why do boy pumpkins wear blue bow-ties?
So you can tell them from girl pumpkins.

What's yellow and sweet and holds
baby monkeys?
An ape-ricot.

What's yellow, furry and rides along
the sea-shore?
A peach buggy.

What's red and green and wears
boxing gloves?
Fruit punch.

What's brown,
mad and lives in
South America?
A Brazil nut.

What's green
and hairy and
takes aspirin?
*A gooseberry
with a headache.*

What's purple and close to France?
Grape Britain.

What's purple and glows in the dark?
A 100 watt grape.

What's round
and purple
and barks at people?
A Grape Dane.

Who swings through the vines?
Tarzan of the Grapes.

What's purple and 8,000 kilometres long?
The Grape Wall of China.

What's fruity and burns cakes?
Alfred the Grape.

What's purple and burns?
The Grape Fire of London.

What's purple and ruled Russian?
Catherine the Grape.

'Mummy, mummy, there's a man at the door selling honey.'
'Tell him to buzz off.'

What did the mother bee say to the baby bee?
'Don't be naughty, honey, just beehive yourself while I comb your hair.'

Why do bees have sticky hair?
Because they have honey combs.

What are the bees on strike for?
More honey and shorter flowers.

What do bees do with honey?
They cell it.

What did the bee say to the flower?
'Hello, honey.'

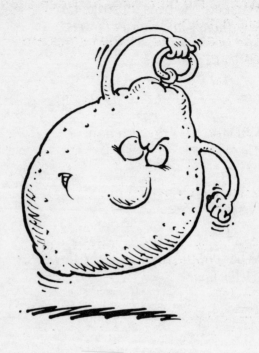

What's yellow and highly dangerous?
A hand grenade disguised as a lemon.

'Holmes, why is that door painted yellow?'
'It's a lemon-entry, my dear Watson.'

What is the difference between a lemon and a melon?
The order in which the letters are written.

How do you make a lemon drop?
Shake the tree.

When a lemon calls for help, what should you give it?
Lemonade

What do you get if you cross a lemon
with a dinosaur?
A dinosour.

What's yellow, sour, and wobbles
all over the road?

A lemon with a puncture.

What did the chicken say when it found
a lemon in the nest?
*'Look at the lemon mama laid
(marmalade).'*

What's furry, whiskered, and sucks
lemons?
A sour puss.

What did the
elephant say
to the lemon?
Let's play squash.

Did you ever see a lemon peel?
No, but I once saw an apple turnover.

What's yellow and flickers?
A lemon with a loose connection.

Knock, knock.
– *Who's there?*
Bab.
– *Bab who?*
Bab Boone is
a real ape.

What do you
call a monkey
with a sweet tooth?
A meringue- outang.

What is the difference between a monkey, a bald man and the Prince of Wales?
A monkey is a hairy parent; a bald man has no hair apparent, and The Prince of Wales is the heir apparent.

Knock, knock.
– *Who's there?*
Beryl.
– *Beryl who?*
Beryl load of monkeys.

What did the monkey say as he fell out of the tree?
Aaarrrggghh!

What does the government use when it takes a census of all the monkeys in the zoo?
An ape recorder!

What do you get
if you cross
a spanner with
a chimpanzee?
A monkey wrench.

What's green and swings through the trees?
A septic monkey.

What keys are furry?
Monkeys.

What do you get if you cross a monkey with a Scottish dance and a joker?
An ape-reel fool.

What do you get
if you cross a
monkey with an idiot?
A chumpanzee.

How do you catch a monkey?
*Hang upside down from a tree and
make a noise like a banana.*

What's the definition of guerilla
warfare?
*Monkeys throwing coconuts at each
other!*

'Is that your own face, or are you
breaking it in for a baboon?'

How do monkeys keep rumours
circulating?
On the apevine.

What's purple
and has
eight legs?
An octoplum.

Who was purple and discovered America in
1492?
Christopher Plumbus.

Who is purple, has scars on his head, and
frightens people?
Frankenplum.

Why is a plum a good museum keeper?
Plum preserves.

What do you
get if you cross
a plum and
a tiger?
*A purple
people eater.*

Which was the smallest plum?
Tom Plum.

What plum wrote under an alias?
Nom de plum.

What is Dracula's favourite pudding?
I scream.

What do climbers eat for dessert?
Rock cakes.

What do you do if
someone offers
you rock cakes
for pudding?
Take your pick.

What's soft and yellow and comes from
outer space?
A martian mellow.

What's the favorite dessert in Wales?
Taffy apples.

What is a lawyer's favorite pudding?
Suet.

What pudding do
you get if you cross
a football team with
an ice cream?
Aston Vanilla.

What do the Scots have for pudding?
Tartan custard.

What's yellow and highly dangerous?
Shark-infested custard.

Knock, knock.
– *Who's there?*
Jaws.
– *Jaws who?*
Jaws truly.

What do you get if you cross an
American president with a shark?
Jaws Washington.

What do you get if you cross a pop
singer with a shark?
Boy Jaws.

What do you get if you cross a shark
with a padlock?
Lock-jaws.

What do you get if you cross a shark
with the Loch Ness Monster?
Loch Jaws!

What do you get
if you cross a
shark with a snowman?
Frost-bite.

What happened to the yacht that sank in shark-infested waters?
It came back with a skeleton crew.

What eats its victims two by two?
Noah's shark.

What shark never swims?
A dead one.

'Waiter, waiter,
there's a fly
in my custard!'
*'That's all right,
sir, the spider
will get it.'*

'Waiter, waiter, there's a fly in my
custard!'
*'I know, it's the rotten fruit that attracts
them.'*

'Waiter, waiter, there's a fly in my
custard!'
*If you throw it a pea it will play water
polo.'*

What's yellow
and highly
dangerous?
*A man-eating
duster.*

If a buttercup is yellow, what colour is a hiccup?
Burple.

Did you hear about the Rubik Cube for wallies? *It's yellow on all six sides.*

What do you get when you jump in the Yellow River?
Wet.

Police: What gear were you in at the time of the accident?
Motorist: *A yellow pullover, if it makes any difference.*

What's tall, yellow and smells nice?
A giraff- odil.

What's yellow and sweet and swings from tree to tree?
Tarzipan.

'I suppose your new baby brother is a lovely pink child?'
'No, he's an 'orrible yeller!'

What happened to the frog when he parked on the yellow line?
He got toad away.

'Why is your dog wearing yellow shoes?'
'Because his black ones are at the mender's.'

What's yellow and brown and dances around toadstools?
A brownie with jaundice.

What's yellow, green, blue, purple, brown, black and white, and good on the draw?
A box of crayons.

What colour is a shout?
Yell-oh.

What's small, yellow, and eats cakes?
A yellow dwarf cake-eater.

What's big and yellow and eats rocks?
A giant yellow rock eater.

What leaves yellow footprints all over the
sea-bed?
A lemon sole.

Why do traffic wardens have yellow lines on
their hats?
To stop people from parking on their heads.

A women with a baby in her arms was sitting in a station waiting room, sobbing miserably. A porter came up to her and asked what the trouble was. 'Some people were in here just now and they were so rude about my little boy,' she cried. 'They all said he was ugly.' *There, there, don't cry,* said the porter kindly. *Shall I get you a nice cup of tea?* 'Thank you, that would be nice,' replied the woman, wiping her eyes. 'You're very kind.' *That's all right. Don't mention it,* said the porter. *While I'm at it, by the way, would you like a banana for your gorilla?*

Why did King Kong climb Cleopatra's Needle?
To get his kite.

Where does a gorilla sleep?
Anywhere it wants to.

Why did the gorilla lie in the middle of the path?

To trip up the ants.

What would you get if you cross a gorilla with a bell?
A ding-dong King Kong.

What do gorillas sing at Christmas time?
'Jungle bells, Jungle bells . . .'

Why don't
gorillas eat
penguins?
*Because they
can't get the
wrappers
off.*

Why do gorillas scratch themselves?
*Because they're the only ones who
know where they itch.*

What's the difference between a biscuit
and a gorilla?
Ever tried dunking a gorilla?

BOY 1: I'm going to keep this gorilla
under my bed.
BOY 2: *But what about the smell?*
BOY 1: He'll just have to get used to it.

What do you call a gorilla who works as
a car mechanic?
A grease monkey.

What do you call
a gorilla with two
bananas in his ears?
*Anything you like,
because he can't
hear you.*

What do you do if you find a gorilla in
your bed?
Sleep somewhere else.

What is big
and hairy
and flies
at Mach 2?
King Kongcorde.

What is big and hairy and goes round
and round?
A gorilla in a revolving door.

Who rings the bell twice then knocks
down the door?
The Avon gorilla.

JANE: I can trace my ancestry all the
way back to royalty.
JILL: *King Kong?*

Why did King Kong join the army?
He wanted to study gorilla warfare.

What's big and hairy and climbs up the
Empire State Building?
Queen Kong.